Matt,
Enjoy & may you
too always be ~

BECKONED BY WATER:

Called to Other Shores

John Hutchinson

by
John Hutchinson

CONTENTS

WHERE WATER RIPPLES TO ROCKS

CROSSING THE CHOPTANK

TROPICAL AFTERNOON

TO THE SEA

THE SIREN CALL OF OTHER SHORES

Where Water Ripples to Rocks

WHERE WATER RIPPLES TO ROCKS

I went to the forest again today
to find
what had been lost.

You know that forest.

That place remote,
stately,
hushed,
a cathedral
where silence is worshipped,
birds call lightly to their own,
water ripples to rocks,
and deer walk without word.

Where everything is everywhere

and yet stilled
for the heart
to find the sound of its own.

HER RIDE HOME

Asleep on a threaded bed of silk,
the outgoing tide of her pulse,
shallow, ebbing,
pulls her down the river.

Comatose most of the time now,
she drifts deeper, deeper,
calm, steady
under light breeze.

Her children stand watch
with red-cast night lanterns
as the grandchildren below
write letters to send ahead.

They think she is almost ready,
wants to slip away, but
holds on for fear
future too will disappear.

While in the dark, Death
waits patiently
near the other shore,
his small boat untied.

KEEPERS OF THE FIRST FIRE

Last night after the storm struck,
shook the house
in its foundation, and winds
tore trees from their roots,
I sat in the quiet
of this here-and-now darkness
like first-man
huddled in a cave.

Sat there yearning for light
and knew
that time had not erased need,
nor how we all go on day-to-day
as collectors of comfort,
minders of memory,
and like those keepers
of the first fire

live with longing
sewn into leathered hearts.

FISH SALE

The fish I got on sale

that my wife baked with bananas,
that we both quietly left on our plates,
that the cats ignored as well,
that we left outside overnight
in the freezing rain
for the raccoons, possums,
or anything with half-a-taste
for fish,

was so bad
that it was still there in the morning
filleted, white-cold,
frozen to the pavement

but the bananas were gone.

FOOTPRINTS

I always wanted to write this poem.

Recapture '78,
the Triple Crown chase,
Affirmed and Alydar,
neck-and-neck,
sweat glistened,
stilled colors flying
down the homestretch,
pounding the turf,
Kentucky, Maryland, New York.

And us, 9 and 37,
our triple-crowned hearts
beating as son and father,
shoulder-to-shoulder,
bare chests heaved to the blue,
you as Affirmed, me as Alydar,
our races down the beach,
the low tide sands
of Cape Henlopen, Delaware.

The footprints of who we were.

SOMETIMES, JUST A LITTLE

His note arrived on a torn piece of beige paper
with a thanks
for what I had shared with him.
He went on to say he's tried to share
some of himself
and hoped that was enough,
quoting Peter Townshend's lyrics of love,
Just a little is enough.

And, considering *a little*,
how many times
have people been rescued
by a thin rope tossed into a stormy sea,
a faint light on a blizzard filled night,
or maybe a few words
that cracked a wall that wanted to crumble?

Sometimes, if it weren't for a little,
enough wouldn't survive.

RAIN

I

Looking through the mottled windshield
of rain,
an impressionist's silvery pointillism,
everything's hazy –
the car in front of him,
the young boy
dashing through the downpour,

that age of clarity.

II

Sitting in the car
after leaving
the doctor's office
rain splattered the windshield,
ran every which way

like answers
that couldn't find their questions.

SELFISHLY

Fishing and down to their last beer,
not catching a thing,
just drowning worms, talking,
remembering old times.

He flicks his cigarette
into the coming glow of darkness,
clears his throat,
says he still remembers.

That night with her
when she led him up the stairs,
wanted them to bathe first, gently
come together.

He was impatient, hungry
for the hard feel of his mouth on hers,
his hand sliding down,
under that thin film of fabric.

Hungry, impatient, and it happened
just the way he wanted.

Now, selfishly, he wonders
how it might have been her way.

UNDER SEA

*(Written for a young man aboard a nuclear submarine
for six months under sea, and only permitted one 50-word message
each week. Inclusive of the title, fifty words were written in his honor.)*

Thomas, turned sailor

surrendered, smiled
to nuclear finned, steel whale

and sank into the sea
where only leviathans dare go.

O, Thomas, we who fear
depths, wonder what pulls you
into the crystalline dark

and wonder too
will you dream the great dream,
the one we dared not?

ON A SILENT, SUDDEN SEA

Do you remember when it was,
what age you were,
the time of day,
or if it was
in the startling blackness of night

when immortality and mortality
passed
on a silent, sudden sea?

Did one not believe the other possible?
Did the other weep for the one passing by?

Or, did their eyes
turn to the pulling sails
so not to see?

MASTERS OF DISGUISE

She quietly mentions the CAT scan,
the visit
to revisit metastasized cells,
and *Hope to be there next Wednesday,*
pretend
that everything's okay, which
I'm becoming
most proficient at, aren't we all?

Yes, he thought, how we all go on
pretending

while Rome burns,
New Orleans drowns, toilets run,
and man hungers

for want of love.

THE CAR

The eleven-year-old, low mileage, garage kept car
bought from my brother,
meticulously kept,
maintained on schedule,
oil changed every three thousand miles,
vacuumed weekly,
waxed every fourth Sunday,
hardly taken out in the rain,
never driven to the ocean where salt air lived

now sat in *my* garage
in fear.

WITNESS

Death and Love

move
like trout
through the deep pool'd mystery
of our days

ready to strike
at a hunger of their own.

ON A FAR-AWAY SEA

Come on in, she said. *He's downstairs*
sleeping.

No, don't worry about that.
He'd be disappointed
if he knew you stopped by
and he didn't get to see you.

Downstairs
in the pine paneled den he built
with his paintings on the walls,
antlers from deer he'd shot,
and his wrap-around bar in the corner,
he lay on his sickbed, a mattress
on the floor
with quilted blanket tucked to chin.

I kneeled, kissed the forehead
of my old friend
who looked up
with a thin face'd smile and eyes
that told the story of his time.

Eyes on a far-away sea
that once held
yesterdays
as if there'd always be tomorrows.

ACROSS AN EARLY MORNING SKY

Gathering cumulous clouds boomed
over the horizon
as the sun not yet risen
gave hint of its coming
with a gentle pink washing
of the eastern sky.

In this dawn light
seven brown pelicans, silhouetted,
etched in beautiful formation,
lifted,
flew out across the ocean.

It was then he saw the B-17s,
that early morning mission,
February 13, 1945.

Dresden.
The hells of fire.

BELOW SEA LEVEL

He peered down
through the porthole of every protection.

They stared up
in dismal disbelief from a watery wasteland.

He did a fly-by at 1700 feet.
They sank lower.

Katrina.
All in despair.

He for his ratings.
They for their lives.

RE-ENTRY

Returning from a ten-day vision quest,
the last four fasting on water,
praying, and wandering
the wilderness of weightlessness,
he headed for home.

With heat shield burnt off and soft
underbelly exposed,
he hurtled down Route 91, past
meteor-sized SUVs,
neon Medusas with wayward song,
and billboards
ablaze with promises of bliss.

Screaming toward re-entry, scrambling
for Band-Aids,
deep breathing exercises,
or anything the deep black cosmos
could offer,

anything he cried,
to keep a man from turning to stone.

FEARLESS

For the nights of those ten days
spent in the Green Mountain National Forest,

home to moose
moving through thicket,
bear he never did see
but thought about,
beaver waddling from water
to where he made his bed,
and other creatures
breaking the wooded sticks of his night,

he slept simply out in the open
with tarp tied to tree
and sleeping bag upon the ground.

Then, for his first night out of the woods
and into a motel,
he closed the door, threw the deadbolt,
and hooked the chain latch

just to be sure.

ON A HORSE WITH HEART

He knew
that vision quest dream
of the weathered Indian woman on horseback,

the woman
determined to pull travois with small child
bundled in basket of stick
across thorn-harsh, rock-filled terrain
where stream beds
had long gone dry,

was him
with that small child tucked inside
trying to get home

on a horse with heart.

ROAD CUT

Driving the mountains of central Pennsylvania,
through a road cut
of aged Appalachian rock,
strata of interbedded stone, folded synclines,
and through layers of recorded time,
the late Permian into an early Triassic period,
70 million years before
the first dinosaurs crawled from the sea,

it all lay exposed

this violent chapter of mountain making,
this time of enormous compressional stresses,
the collision of continental plates,
and the heat
that bent the earth to its knees

like love.

COFFEE, TWO EGGS OVER EASY

I was in Idaho, Ketchum really,
skiing, exploring,
opening eyes long dormant,
seeing what yesterday
might have walked on by.

The rusted, red
bicycle
axel deep in snow
leaned against a wooden shed.

Those icicles
glistening long and thin, hung
from a high-pitched
tin roof.

That waitress in the old
mining town café,
her tired blonde hair, her early
morning smile, greeting,

Whadda ya have, bud?

THE SCENT OF SEX

There along the creek bank
of the Yampa River
was the young, inviting,
bronzed,
bare-breasted woman,
lying
with her back arched,
her arms open
to the falling snow.

Cast in the scent of sex,
the sculptor knew
how to make heat rise
on a cold day.

MINDLESSLY LOST

It's Miami, the airport, Chili's-to-Go,
bacon-cheeseburger on order,
van ride in an hour,
then Key Largo to Key West,
follow Henry Flagler's
100-year-old railroad to paradise.

But, instead of steel rail
a kayak will part the turquoise sea
with a man,
one paddle stroke after the other,
mindlessly paddling
on wind and wave
as saltwater splashes over the bow.

A man lost in a paddle stroke mantra
under a blue-eyed sky
in a meditation so deep
the Buddha
would be bowed with envy.

ALMOST OVER

It's almost over, Key Largo to Key West,
one-hundred-fifteen miles,
the anticipation, worry, and even regret
I begin to feel upon leaving
friends found in the common soup
of chaos and calm
where kayaks tossed and rocked
over the turbulent seas of the Keys
and too all those days
when sun and sky smiled, gave away
fair blessing of wind and wave.

It's almost over and again I realize
that everything is a metaphor,
that channel we crossed
where wind blew hard against tide
and waves rose high, then
the calm that came.
How everything passes.

It's almost over, our bond over beer,
dirt, water, and time.
Soon we'll reach our destination
and depart to old lives, days
predictably dressed in the faded color
of routine, days that will drag along
until we look to the horizon

and begin to yearn again.

Crossing the Choptank

CROSSING THE CHOPTANK

Driving Route 50, crossing the Choptank
that day returned.

How my father came into the kitchen
with fish
caught from that river,
dropped their cold slabs into the sink,
stood there, scraped scales,
and quietly cleaned the catch.

How I wished that day returned
just to see him again, ask questions
I never got around to asking.

I wouldn't ask what it's like
on the other side or even for answers
to this worn and riddled life.

I'd just want to ask, *How was it that*
cold, November day? What did you catch?
Was the captain stern, his word law?

How did you keep your hands warm
handling wet fish? How was it decided
to end this frigid day of fishing?

Dad, I'd say, *I want all the details,*
leaving nothing out, all you remember,
to help me remember.

THE RIVER

Quiet
collects the overhanging canopy,
green that mirrors up on down,
the great northern cypress,
knees held high and pink and dry,
the swamp azalea
that gives itself freely to the fragrance of air.

Quiet
gathers in the skipper
that tip-toes needle-black across the water,
the prothonotary's warble,
a golden, sweeted song for the verdant woods.

Quiet
embraces the slow winding river,
whispers

Pocomoke.

EARL AND STANLEY NORMAN
(An old-time sonnet for a waterman and his boat)

While captain, cook, and crew took hand to oar,
an old black man stayed back upon the boat.
As others took their leave to head to shore
just Earl and *Stanley Norman* stood afloat.

Both man and boat, well-weathered, worn with age,
at eighty-three and ninety-nine they knew
an ebbing tide made time a fading page
so twenty years of oak and blood stayed true.

Now Earl and boat ne'er once did say that day
how crab and clam, the cold month oysters caught,
the seas of calm, the storms that blew the Bay,
how heave and ho on halyards pulled they wrought.

T'was skipjack, raking mast of yellow pine,
and Earl at peace, well-anchored in his time.

BEQUEATHED

Driving Route 50 along the Eastern Shore,
past the green road signs
for Hurlock and Secretary,
near where James Michener moved
to live this rural life and write
his epic *Chesapeake,*
the memory of that book returned.

The one I found for 50-cents
on the used book rack
of the Ocean City Public Library
with *Elmira Van Collom*
handwritten inside the front cover.

The gift of a book I gave to my wife
with
her long deceased mother's name
written inside.

TIDYING UP THE SHED

With eyes of fire and jaw set to concrete,
he strode from the woods
onto the beach, white-naked
but for the brown shorts and six-inch
hunting knife, determined
to do the work a man is called to do.

He stepped into the sloshing surf
where the dead loggerhead turtle lay
with trophy shell
big as his wife's washbasin.
He cut, sawed, and took one leg,
then another, pulled on the intestines,
long as his wife's clothesline.
And, knelt in the swirled, bloodstained
water and took knife to the bill-faced,
barnacled, black-eyed head

the nagging voice that said
he kept an untidy shed.

CAMPFIRE TALK

I

The secret, he grinned
as he held the unwashed pot for us to see,
*to making good coffee
is to always leave behind some grinds
for the next pot.*

And the coffee was,
on our unshaven mornings,
always good.

II

With hands twice the size of mine

hands that looked like they'd been forged by God
to do the work of the ages,
hands tanned, heavily knuckled, muscled
to look as if they could have built the Sistine Chapel
and painted the ceiling art as well.

He said his arthritis was bothering him too.

LEFT IN THE WAKE

"Everyone, as the phrase goes, knows two things about Alexander...
he was the man who wept because there were no more worlds to
conquer, and he was the man who 'cut the knot'."
                                    W.W. Tarn, *Alexander the Great*

After three days of paddling the Chesapeake,
the wind, the wave, the insistent voice
of the present moment,
the rhythmic calls to attention,

the Gordian knot carried inside, the one
that knew no beginning nor end,
nor where anger wound tight to angst,
or where want had strung wish to wart,

all was left in the wake,
cut by the sword of NOW.

THE SEA HE SO LOVED TO SAVE
(In memory of Philip Merrill)

Champion for a Chesapeake Bay National Park,
advocate for the *Save the Bay Foundation,*
this son of a Russian immigrant,
Baltimore rowhouse boy,
sailor at age seven,
editor of his college newspaper,
graduate of Cornell University,
merchant marine,
U.S. State Department employee,
Export-Import Bank chairman,
tempered, blustery.

This newspaper owner-publisher,
diplomat, philanthropist,
husband, father
put from port that morning
in his *Merrilly* painted sailboat
the aqua color of his love,
the sea he surged across on sails
bellowed by wind,
the sea he so loved to save

which took him
in a final embrace that day.

TWELVE KAYAKS

We leaned forward, parted the Chesapeake
for three days,
peeled back layer after layer
of shimmered green
through stinging, splashed
saltwater to the eyes.

With heads cocked right
watching for beam-reaching seas
and with faces firmly fixed
to grin or terror,
we paddled into a future
where it never mattered so much
where we were going

it only mattered we were going.

THE CREEK OF THE FULL MOON RISING

"...heaven and earth have never
agreed better to frame a place for man's habitation..."
Captain John Smith, 1612

The first stop of Captain John Smith's voyage
into the Chesapeake Bay
is now our last stop
as we paddle this late afternoon
into the clear water and quiet sanctuary
of Old Plantation Creek.

On this creek of the full moon rising
we start fire and make camp
for rest,
swim, food, drink,
and sunset.

O' Captain, four hundred years
and let me tell you
heaven and earth still agree.

LOST AND IN LOVE WITH NOTHING

Crossing the new Choptank River bridge,
the old bridge still stands.

It's a fishing pier of sorts where the poor
gather, lean against the rail
with rod in hand or the rod leaned
against the railing.
Some folks sit on folding chairs
or upturned buckets,
some have umbrellas, some have
bicycles leaned nearby,
most everyone is stationary,
most are black or oriental.
The day is summer-August-still. Hot.

Driving by,
I wonder what they're thinking.
Are they wishing for a bite, a fish,
a change of luck,
or maybe just getting a break,

lost and in love with nothing.

WHAT I SAW
(Tornado, Savage Neck, Virginia -- June 1, 2012.)

As the storm raged, gale force winds howled,
thunder clapped, and lightning
ripped apart a nighttime sky,
the driven rain drenched the kayakers
huddled under a whipping
beach-spread tarp.

It was the faces seen, still recalled,
caught
in the fierce, continuing
strobe light flashes in the blackness of night.

Faces frozen
to the changing moments of being fully alive --
fear,
ecstasy,
terror,
maybe surrender too.

ODE TO THE EASTERN SHORE

You wear your days without pretense,
lie flat without worry for a hill,
cloak yourself in cornfields, an everyday shade
of green.

Burn your grass to a late summer tan,
stand unshuttered in two-story white,
walk your telephone poles down to meet the horizon.

Dot your roads with produce stands,
graze unworried deer at the edge of fields, and slowly
you carry away the names of your ancestors,
Nanticoke and Pocomoke.

Eastern Shore,
you wear boring like a regal mark of beauty.

THE WATERMAN
(for Allan Smith of Tylerton and other watermen of the Chesapeake)

Awakes to a black pearl, early morning sky,
shuffles to skiff, motors across creek to crab shanty,
sorts and packs soft-shells for market
while water trickles from the shedding trays.

Boards Hester Lee, pulls heavy slickers over pants,
shrugs broad shoulders under suspenders,
tugs rubber gloves over toil-thickened hands,
stows a brown, paper bag lunch
as the sky to the east begins to break.

Turns the switch,
coughs an engine to life, a throaty sound that carries far on water,
tosses mooring lines, eases the workboat away from dock,
motors to find the grass-bed fishing grounds he trusts,
drops an iron scrape astern, begins dredging,
plowing the sea in search of crab.

Bends to the first pull of the day,
strains to bring heavy iron scrape to boat,
dumps the catch on the culling board, sorts and tosses
while seeming not to look – sooks, Jimmies,
buckrams, peelers to this basket or that,
small ones cast back to Bay.

His day is art and grace – a wooden boat
of crab basket clutter, rusted hatchet, sun-cracked life ring,
discarded plastic bottles, scent of the sea
seasoned with motor oil, hypnotic thrum of engine,
a weathered man of 70 in crimson cap
bent to his work.

Wheeling, crying gulls following behind.

OFFSHORE

I want to tell you how it was that day.

How they arrived
shedding the sea from their backs,
rhythmically rising and falling,
offering their shiny, black moon eyes to me.

How they rose from the green hold of the sea
barely a fathom or two away,
released held breath,
then slipped sinuously away.

Then, rose again by the side of my kayak,
or slid under keel, or followed along
with slight twist of tail,
and how it was so magically mysterious.

Like I said, I wanted to tell you
how it was that day,
and how it is we sometimes get a glimpse
of delight

ours and maybe another's.

Tropical Afternoon

TROPICAL AFTERNOON

Her face
fell from the fronds of the palm.
His fingers
trembled to unbutton the blouse.

The boat under sail, bellied by wind
slid through the opening in the reef,
rose high on the mounting swells of the sea,
fell hungry upon the horizon.

The tropical bird
shrieked from the throat of longing.
The stilled iguana
stared warmth into the sun.

IN FLIGHT

I

Below
lights sprinkle the dark,

houses
peopled with dreams, despair, TVs droning, bills
to pay, faucets dripping, taxes to do,

beds stained with sex
hoping for love.

II

In flight
with an empty reach of blue above,
matted white clouds below, and the platinum eye
of the sun piercing the window,
we slid through the sky at 35,000 feet.

The ease of some things we do.

And knowing what we hold on to
weights us down and what we release lifts us,
why do we go on swimming like golden carp
in a drowning sea?

SONG FOR MARIANO

Each day you walked the beach
with shy and downcast eye
and pulled along the wide,
blue Sayulitan sky.

Oh, native boy of brown
you didn't go to school,
but came instead with craft
you made from hand and tool.

My Huichol Indian child
from mountain home you walked.
You knew that snakes brought rain,
that deer and wolf could talk,

and arrows carried prayer.
You came each day with tray,
your beadwork, painted shell,
and masks. But, best I say

my grandson's quiet smile.

THE BRIDGE OF SURRENDER

They came quietly to a small house
by the edge of the sea,
sat in white, plastic chairs,
a circle of stored stories
of the cell's longing
and the soul's bottled up journey.

Their stories came out one by one,
Hi, I'm ....

Only first names were given
because last names didn't matter
only the truth
lying behind a worn facade of identity.

The stories poured out, twisted
tales of torment
caught in the curse of craving,
riddled with remorse and resistance

all traveling
over the bridge of surrender
to hope.

AT ROSY'S

There's no door,
just a green gate swung open for the day,
a courtyard with thatch roof,
four white tables of plastic
as well the chairs,
and the Puerto Morelos ocean breeze.

On this warm, late afternoon,
a round, brown woman with skillet, stove,
and reluctant smile cooks,
a gray cat curls against the wall,
a thin, brown dog wanders through,
a blind boy hums, head-bobs
to CD'd Christmas carols,
and a pony-tailed Mexican nods
for another glass of wine.

Rosy, in tight sequined jeans, loose
white blouse, moving
with the music,
smiles, slides toward his table.

HAUNTED

I didn't sleep well last night. Was reading
and got caught up
in the drama
that hit a bit too close to home.

I knew it was just a story
like any other story, maybe yours or mine,
filled with love, loss, lust, remorse
and wrapped in the condition
called human,
a story as old as the ages
where only the characters change.

I knew it, but still had trouble
letting go. Finally,
as the clock trudged past midnight
I fell asleep.

Isn't that the way it always is,
the stories we hang on to haunt us?

OFFSHORE REEF

In the distance,
maybe no more than a mile offshore,
waves appear,
    swell,
        roll,
            break white
                over the reef,
then are swallowed
back into the sea again.

That reef,
mostly unseen, built by coral,
cell by cell,
living, growing, multiplying
over the years into an undersea mountain

like memories
built by the stone of thought,
piled one onto the other
of their own need to be remembered.

LIKE CELLS IN A SINGULAR ORGANISM

Packed tight on the plane, every seat taken,
even the aisle crowded with cart.

Somehow I feel strangely at one
with this bunch:
the bent, elderly oriental woman,
the black with chains hanging from his waist,
the muscle'd man in tank top and tattoos,
the pert young girl budding her breasts,
the homely woman next to me
          munching a bar of dark chocolate,
even myself.

Like cells in a singular organism
we swim our way across a common sky
sinking into a sunset.

Sometimes, I wonder why
I avoid, can't stand, and seek isolation
from this humanly mass.

Sometimes with a glass of wine
we're almost tolerable.

BAJA, FROM 24,000 FEET

Brown, wrinkled,
ragged,
at times peaked in white,
coursed by stream beds
      long gone dry,
aged, peninsula'd,
surrounded by supple seas
      of leviathans.

A land
aching, thirsting
for whatever the gods
      will give,

maybe
even love.

MORNING COFFEE

Cold! It was so cold last night
I woke, rooted
around in my tent, put on
fleece socks, hat, and Capilene
long underwear.
Then, burrowed back
into my sleeping bag, curled
into a fetal position,
and cuddled myself back to sleep.

But, by 8:20 in the morning
it was back to t-shirt, shorts, sandals,
and sunglasses
on a Baja desert day already hot
with the sea still and nothing moving
except for the flies,

even the dead one
I spit from my coffee.

WHERE SECRETS ARE HELD

Another cold day drizzles by
outside my April window, but inside
the Baja desert returns. Then,
the breeching, sounding
whales of Magdalena Bay.

The whales, who knows
why they came,
why a mother allowed her baby
nuzzle so close,
offer barnacled head,
down-turned, baleen filled mouth
to reaching,
touching, caressing hands.

I only know why I came
and how mystery
still lies in the depths of all of us
where secrets are held,
sometimes released

to the touch of another's hand.

To the Sea

TO THE SEA

Finally, we arrive in Belize
where our kayak expedition will begin,
where the sun has eased down,
and where silhouetted palms
lean between us and the horizon
and all that is left behind --
those weary ways of days
worn with crowded highways,
politicians spinning truth
for the gods of greed,
and the endless wars upon a people
thirsting only
for a lasting taste of peace.

Now, we are among those
who talk an easy talk,
live by a sea that never wanted
to be anything but sea,
and where the cormorant too
knows the path of least resistance,
flies downwind
just above the rippled waves.

Tomorrow, we will hear the ocean say,
Come, and we will go.

Give ourselves to the sea.

LOST

After ten days paddling the islands of Belize,
time was lost.
Days and dates had disappeared.

Hours crawled away on the back of the hermit crab
that inched across the sand,
minutes were conquered by the dusty black dog
curled under the table,
seconds were swallowed
by the crystalline, blue-green sea,
and the sun wore away
the tired old hands of the clock
while the trade winds
carried away everything else.

Tell me, what did time look like?
Do you remember?

FIVE MILES OUT

Jamaal says, *Yes, mon, we'll go fishin' again toodey.*

Now, this was after yesterday's fierce catch
of a howling squall
that blew his kayak away from mine,
downwind,
down rolling green waves,
down through the torment of time,
and through a gap in a patch reef
      into a place of calm
where I finally caught my breath.

Looking around I saw the storm had passed
and I was alone
on a sea larger than I wanted to see.

Jamaal says we'll go fishing again today.

THE CHICKEN DINNER THAT WAITED

While the frigate birds slowly swirled away
the last of a blue evening sky,
Damasco was asked, *Hey,*
are you from these parts? Standing there
with chicken in one hand
and knife in the other, he answered.

Yes, mon, I am. You know, my great grandfather,
Thomas Vincent Ramos
founded Settlement Day in Belize.
It's November 19th, de day de Garifuna people
first landed der boats in dis country.
Every year we select a queen who must sing,
dance de punta, answer questions,
and tell a story in de native language.
It's an important time and we eat de traditional foods.
Dere is much drumming and dancing.

Then, quietly the chicken was slid
back onto the table, but the knife gestured on,

You know, it's a time of much happening.
We have brujos who can cast spells,
send people into a trance. I once saw a man
who was so rooted four men couldn't lift him
from de ground. We had to get another brujo
to get de spell removed.
De spells are real, mon, I tell you dey're real!

HERON

Her highness glides,
slides her slow, low tide steps,
patiently pursues,
stops,
points her prey,

spears

a silent, circled ripple.

JACK AND MANADI
(Manadi, Mayan for manatee. Or, if you will, sea cow.)

He sailed in on the setting sun.
Shook my hand.
Said his name was Jack, Jack Wilde.
Tied his blue-white boat to a tree,
a craft splotched Holstein-like
with black epoxy paint.

Said his patched, 17-foot sailboat
was named *Manadi*. Homemade.
Built from a Garifuna
dugout canoe. Had an outrigger
of plank, Styrofoam, and fiberglass.
Had spar and mast of local mangrove.

Said he wouldn't be staying long.
Would sail on to Nicaragua,
then head up-river.
Catch a ride on a pickup
to the Pacific, then sail home
to San Carlos in Sonora, Mexico.

Jack, standing in the setting sun
next to his beloved Manadi,
sporting a red-beard, pony-tail,
torn Hawaiian shirt, and the blue
sparkle for an eye,
truly was a holy shit moment.

TELL ME

What is it worth to lie on your back
and see stars
brighter than ever before,
hear the lap of the night-time sea
by the flap of your tent,
and know
the next day you will wake again
to turquoise
as the bed beneath your kayak
while the frigate birds
paint black
across the blue of one more sky?

CONCH FISHERMAN

Eight miles offshore from the Garifuna
town of Dangriga,

protected in fiberglass kayaks
with waterproof hatches,
clothed and hatted
in the latest weather garments,
smeared with #30 sunscreen,
and wearing
a Coast Guard approved life preserver,

we see a local fisherman,
his sinuous, ebony body
rise from the sea,
toss a conch into his dugout canoe,
climb in,
and paddle off with handmade
wood paddle,

buoyed
by the wide, white grin of a smile.

BREAKFAST TALK

When the local fellow paused in filleting a papaya,
he was asked about cats, *Freeman,*
where are the cats? We don't see many.

Oh yes, mon, over in Dangriga
we hab plenty. I had two, but de rats
beat dem up all de time.
Once I locked de cats up in de ceiling
but de rats went up dere
and beat dem up again. Dey're bush rats.
We call dem coconut squirrels too.
Once I saw a rat peel a coconut,
make a hole, den eat everyding inside.

Freeman, standing there in plastic flip flops,
orange shirt, corn-rowed smile,
and the turquoise sea at his back,
went on,

We also hab dogs and chickens in our house,
but dey get along okay.

The Siren Call of Other Shores

THE SIREN CALL OF OTHER SHORES

Sorrento brought the fragrance of lemon,
grapes on the vine,
hills of olive, an agreeable climate,
houses chiseled into cliffs,
winding streets, pint sized cars,
nary a red light, Italian pasta,
pleasant people, attractive women,

and cruise ships to taste these delights.

Seduced too as was Ulysses
who stopped the ears of his crew with wax
and then was tied to the mast
to resist the siren call of other shores.

He never knew what he missed.

ISLE OF CAPRI

Surrounded by a cerulean sea,
the Herculean arms of the Gulf of Naples,
and only two-by-four in miles,
but rising precipitously into the sky,
Capri was a beautiful adventure
of skinny roads,
fat buses, and overfed tourists.

Climbing these cliff-side roads
our driver didn't help when he said,
Here, only the good
and the dead drivers remain.

So, we said our little prayers
as we climbed the dizzying heights,
made our way to the summit,
tasted the pizza,
drank the beer, ate gelato,
and took in scenery so stunning
it was simply a view to kill for,

this one-time home of Benito Mussolini.

WHILE HIS NIGHTS RAN WILD

Leaving David standing in his marbled grace
of Florence,
we drove on to Venice
minding the white lines on the roads,
paying attention to green mileage markers,
and too,
the yellow signs advising caution.

That's when David came to mind again.

How he drove his armies righteously
to conquer the Jebusites
while his nights ran wild in Jerusalem
as Bathsheba
bathed in the courtyard below.

THE CHARIOT DRIVER

There at Circus Maximus

cloaked in royal Roman red,
hammered bronze helmet,
amulet of golden brass,
imported steel sword,
sandaled too
in the latest Armani leather,

wielding
whip and carrot,

frothing at the mouth,
wild with wide eye,
coursing sweat,

the horse
had no idea
what was wrong with this man.

FROM THE DEPTHS OF THE PERUVIAN SEA

Three poems arrived
as dreams
in the dark of a Cusco night
like incandescent little fishes
from the depths of the Peruvian Sea
curious and expectant
to see and be seen.

Then, having done
what they were wont to do,
disappeared
on the flit of a fin,
leaving me
to tell their tale.

FIRST NIGHT IN CUSCO

The cruelty of the poem is that she often
arrives in the midst of the night
like a restless lover
banging upon your door,
demanding entrance,
refusing to be denied,
insisting she be yours
and only yours,
heaving her fiery breath
upon your chest,

then comes

to leave you
with what you bring to tomorrow.

PERU, PERU

Last night you came, banged your words
upon my bed.

Why did you come to me, give fishes
        from the cold breath of your sea,
pour your poor
        upon the hills of hope,
send that shy brown smile
        from under the lip of her hat,
turn my ears to the Quechua
        hungering for their tongue to be heard,
raise the stone stairway
        to the Gate of the Sun,
wave your red flag of chichi,
        give drink to the weary of the road?

Why did you erase your Shining Path,
        the promise of a promise lost,
lift the weight of your people
        with a branch of cocoa leaf,
lay terraced hills dormant
        in wait for a king,
walk school children miles
        to give away ruddy-faced smiles,
and cry your glacial tears,
        release the soul of the Andes to me?

Peru, Peru,
why did you waken me?

LUANG PRABANG

It almost could have been anywhere.

Golden-eyed trucks pierce the dark.
The moon bulges toward full.
A rooster ratchets the edge of dawn.
Wood smoke drifts across the road.
Tuk-tuks prowl early for fares.
Dust hangs on moist morning air.
The temple drum beats a slow call.
Monks walk to silent meditation.

A silent passerby nods, *Sa bi dee*.

As I said
it almost could have been anywhere
in this subtropical world
of Southeast Asia, but this time
it was in Laos, in a small city
awakening
in the mist of the Mekong.

.

FOR THE PAIN OF IT
(Written at the request of my Cambodian guide.)

Love, even the evil Ravana,
the demon king in the Hindu epic, *Ramayana*,
had more than a speck of it in his heart.

Smitten with love for the already betrothed
Sita,
Ravana stole her away from the God-King Rama.
But Rama,
with Hanuman's mighty army of monkeys,
crossed the bridge of the sea
and cross-bowed Ravana in the heart that cared.

Love, how one can die from the pain of it.

TO THE SEA AGAIN

Why not go to the sea again,
give yourself, all of you, ask no favor,
abandon conditional love,
take all she offers
as she only asks the same of you?

Why not go where harsh and beautiful
live side by side, where unnecessary
is shed, the North Star
beats wildly in the heart,
and where you are one with water?

Why not part the shimmered sea,
lean into the face of wind and wave,
bend into gale, know fear,
immensity, smile to being fully alive
inside this small life of you?

Why not go to that other shore,
push beyond,
travel to where truth lives and knows
no other name,
where even the sorest heart is restored?

Go. Go to the sea, read storied clouds,
sleep with ear to singing shores,
wake to a new light. Walk to where
others gather by fire, pour your coffee,
taste the gift of this new day.

Made in the USA
Charleston, SC
31 October 2012